LEFTOVERS

LEFTOVERS

JOHN H. MACDONALD

Leftovers

Copyright © 2019 by John H. Macdonald. All rights reserved.

No part of this publication may be reproduced, stored in a retrieval system or transmitted in any way by any means, electronic, mechanical, photocopy, recording or otherwise without the prior permission of the author except as provided by USA copyright law.

The opinions expressed by the author are not necessarily those of URLink Print and Media.

1603 Capitol Ave., Suite 310 Cheyenne, Wyoming USA 82001
1-888-980-6523 | admin@urlinkpublishing.com

URLink Print and Media is committed to excellence in the publishing industry.

Book design copyright © 2019 by URLink Print and Media. All rights reserved.

Published in the United States of America

ISBN 978-1-64367-783-5 (Paperback)
ISBN 978-1-64367-782-8 (Digital)

16.07.19

A FATEFUL LOOK

You looked at me and all was lost, my heart was beating strong.
A treasured smile, a devious laugh, my fortitude was gone.
We talked awhile and later on, we met and had a drink.
The fevered pitch of destiny, hold on, I have to think.
I took you home, we said goodnight and there was the beginning.
A sleepless night, I tossed and turned, my thoughts had turned to sinning.
I called you up and finally asked if you would like to dine.
I never took the time to think, my word she could be mine.
I held the door as we walked in, admiring her charms.
The slightest touch, it means so much, to hold her in my arms.
The night was young and so were we, the stars were burning bright.
Eventually we realized how this could take all night.
The morning came, the sun arrived and she was still with me.
Thank you God for everything and please just let it be.
You looked at me with sleepy eyes, inquiring the time.
It didn't matter any way, just as long as you were mine.
The storybook, a fateful look, a date with destiny.
Your smiling face, I can't replace, please come along with me.
The time has passed, the years are gone and you are somewhere else.
And I am still remembering, alone and by myself.
The fateful look, the one I took will last eternally.
A strident voice, my final choice, I guess I'll let it be.
Somewhere in time, when you were mine, I know this much is true,
The fateful song of destiny, I'm still in love with you.

A FULL MOON RISING

Behold as the darkened shadows are overcome with a full moon rising. The cascading light reveals a sleeping world, unaware of what the forthcoming day has in store. Somewhere in the shadows lye the idle seeds of destiny unknown to the adventurous souls now awakened. With a touch of wind, the slightest breeze, the beneficent hand of mother earth reaches out and fertilizes the trees, the flowers, the perpetual fruits we know so well. Her gentle touch a refreshing promise of another day. Arise again you sleepy souls, the morning sun is now upon us. Such an appealing feeling, berift of mourning and emboldened by the early spring, we cherish and welcome the all powerful hand of God. With artistic fervor the bread of life is offered and a drink of wine that soothes the soul.

Another day of apathy. Another bout with destiny. The winners rise, the losers fall and here we stand, but most of all, the tears we shed for fallen brothers, the love we share with one another. A blissful night becomes the dawn, a righteous plan too soon is gone. The angels high above us sing, the love of God for all to bring. The poets words, a trusting sound, another day will come around. A message sent for us to hear, a morning dove to make it clear. A trusting hand to till the field, the touch of Him is now revealed.

Behold as a full moon rising, the gift of light overshadows the apathy of man. This is not a world of me, no this cannot be. The world is our orchard, a fruitious blend of harmony, a becoming song of destiny. Ours is to pick and choose. The alternative is for us to lose. As raindrops shield us from the sun, our time on earth is now begun. We lift a glass and sing a toast to Him we love The Holy Ghost.

ADAM @ EVE

Somewhere lost in time and written down in the fabric of history, you will find the story of Adam @ Eve. In the tongues of so many different cultures and dialects are the iconic words that define the past and future of humanity. And to think it all revolves around a flowering apple tree. According to the most famous forms of literature, these two young and innocent individuals, happened upon a tree bearing a fruit that became the most famous of all, an apple which I would guess, was a Delicious. She reached out and ripped one down, took a bite, well I would bet they shared a bite and all hell became a part of human destiny. What they didn't see, or perhaps chose to ignore was the snake from hell who inspired, or perhaps enthusiastically offered a reason to ignore the rules of the forbidden fruit. All of a sudden they were no longer comfortable with their naked feelings of proper habits and apparel. Both the appetite for apples and something more, something new and overpowering and that would be desire. I dare say, the vast majority of humanity have taken a bite and suffered just like their ancestors and still have not learned the lessons of history. We all cannot resist this temptation, never could and never will. I am familiar with this sense of guilt, more than once and yet, if God had not provided these feelings of desire, of sexuality, where would we be? Would we be still searching for the meaning of humanity, a reason for existence itself? Who would we be questioning and who would have the answers? And thus was born the essence of religious beliefs. Many have walked the sands of time, searching and preaching about the hand of God, prolific and overpowering, dynamic and irrefutable.

So, my question would be, what have we learned from the history of Adam @ Eve? Is humanity still searching? What are we supposed to have learned from their experiences? Are we, collectively so stupid or ignorant to face the truth about who we are or what has become of a sense of humility to God and man himself? The truth be known, we all suffer from vanity, which becomes all too often, a loss of propriety and leads us right back to the apple tree. I truly enjoy a Delicious apple now and then, don't you?

ANGEL

There is an Angel in the distance, far away from me,
We never met, at least not yet, a girl I long to see.
On the phone when we have spoken, a voice I like to hear,
A precious sound, at last I've found, polite and so sincere.
A man of words, perhaps you've heard, she's helped me with my books.
So far away, perhaps I'll stay, a victim of her looks.
In a perfect place, my Angels face, will light up every room,
Perhaps we'll dance, a new romance beneath a winters moon.
A pleasant song, please come along and spend some time with me.
A lonely night, a pure delight, a date with destiny.
There is an Angel in the distance, far away from here,
A night complete, with kisses sweet, come to me my dear.
A vision of tomorrow, or later on tonight,
Her lovely charms, held in my arms, a heavenly delight.
I know a lovely Angel, a sound so loud and clear,
Until at last I meet her, I'll still be waiting here.

AT THE END OF THE DAY

At the end of the day, what do I see?
The girl of my dreams somehow waiting for me.
At the end of the day, when I'm thinking of you,
With all the girls I have known, all the things we could do.
At the end of the day, as I lay in my bed,
I'm still thinking of you and all the things that you said.
At the end of the day, there's a look in your eyes,
From the first time we touched, there can be no disguise.
At the end of the day, when I can't let you go,
With each beat of my heart, I'm still loving you so.
At the end of the day, when you are at home,
I can't help thinking of you, when I'm all alone.
At the end of the day and I'm trying to sleep,
I'll be dreaming of you, there's a memory to keep.
At the end of the day, all my dreams have come true,
There's no way I could hide, just how much I love you.
At the end of the day and you're still in my head,
I'd rather be holding you, so close in my bed.
At the end of the day, we should be saying goodnight,
Just give me a kiss and I'll turn out the light.
At the end of the day, I'll be holding your hand,
I can't help thinking all the things we have planned.
At the end of the day, there's one more thing I should do,
I'll be yelling out loud, just how much I love you!

BABY IT'S COLD OUTSIDE

Baby it's cold outside,
The wind keeps blowin', the snows been fallin', the ice gets thicker every day.
The clouds are darkened, my tempers sparkin', it's freezin' cold I have to say.
Baby it's cold outside,
The phone stopped ringin', the birds quit singin', this storm will last the whole night through.
Just slipped and fell and then I yelled, don't know what on earth to do.
Baby it's cold outside
I had a thought, let's build a fire, so we can snuggle up together.
We'll stay inside and try to hide from another night of nasty weather.
Baby it's really cold outside.
January's almost done, I used to think all this is fun, but now I'm really not so sure.
February and March are yet to come and more bad weather we must endure.
It's just so darn cold outside
My nose is drippin', we all keep slippin', can't wait for spring to reappear.
These wintry days, won't go away, it seems to happen at least once a year.
Baby it's cold outside,
The snow is drainin', the birds are trainin', I can almost feel my toes.
It's gettin' warmer, the sun is shinin', how this happened no one knows.
Baby it's warmer outside,
The wind's still blowin', the rain is fallin', I guess we have a springtime day.
The garden's growin', the river's flowin', I only hope it's here to stay.

BOY MEETS GIRL

There was a young boy who met a girl, her hair adorned with a slender curl.
He grew up strong into a man, they fell in love and had a plan.
Each day that passed into a year, they still were one and had no fear.
They both relied on what they knew, at last it came, the end of school.
They took a trip down lover's lane, the way they felt was still the same.
There was a church just east of town, they made a vow on Holy ground.
Together they would face the world, the strength of him, her hair uncurled.
She still belonged, held in his arms and he a vision of her charms.
They chose a path both east and west, they're life as one was just a test.
The years have passed, they're older now, the way they feel will last somehow.
They loved and raised a family, for them it was a destiny.
You know that church just east of town, it's holy bell has fallen down.
Another day, another week, the pastor knows of what I speak,
Those lovers lie beneath a stone, the way they felt is still unknown.
But, with the early rising sun, I think they're love has just begun.

DARK SHADOWS

Somewhere in the morning shadows, just before the morning sun,
When the stars are barely visible and another day's begun,
You can hear the robins chirping, as they search the holy ground,
Just don't think about tomorrow and you dare not make a sound.
The fog has barely lifted as you dive into your car,
Just prepare to be offended or you might not get too far.
When the morning sun appears as it comes blazing through the clouds,
You must herald the beginning of what God above allows.
He never said it would be easy a shadowed visage from above.
It was a fated promise of His undivided love.
Somewhere in the evening shadows as the sun begins to fade,
When the stars are shining brighter like the promise that He made,
All around us we see heaven as the rain begins to fall,
It's the mother's milk of nature, a growing fabric for us all.
As I lay me down to sleep, with a vision of tomorrow,
I can dream about what happened with a lonely sense of sorrow.
If only we had listened and gave heed to words now spoken,
We could justify the meaning and his heart would not be broken.
In the early morning shadows just before the breaking dawn,
We must celebrate His love and pray it never will be gone.

DO YOU LOVE ME

Do you love me, I need to know? Do you love me, or should I go?
Do you want me, I'm asking you? I'll do anything you want me to.
Did you ever care, through all those years? I need to know despite my tears.
Do you remember when we kissed? Through those lonely nights, it's you I missed.
We traveled on a midnight train, and late at night it began to rain.
We skied the Rockies on fresh fallen snow, the very next day we had to go.
Do you love me, remember when? And if you would, let's do it again.
I'm asking you with a broken heart, why the hell are we apart?
Just say you want me and if you do, I'll be loving you the whole night through.
Endless days and nights may come and go. Despite the time, I still love you so.
I called you on my new cell phone, I need to know, are you alone?
Should you desire my company, you know it's where I want to be.
Our song keeps ringing in my head, I'd rather be with you instead.
The nights grow longer, it's winter time. I only wish that you were mine.
The rain has stopped, it turned to snow and once again I miss you so.
The sun beams hot, the flowers grow, there's just one thing I need to know.
Do you love me, I need to know and if you do, I'll never go.

EMOTIONS

Emotions are a human reaction not easily put in terms we all understand. Oh, a physician could demonstrate which portion of the brain provides the chemical reaction, which in turn sparks an electric charge, becoming what some would refer to as an emotional response. On the other hand a philosopher might look elsewhere for a more humanistic explanation. He might say the daily world may be run by the mentality of those in charge, but the heart is where the emotional segment of society truly rules. For most of us, the daily regimen of earning a living to provide those items of substance we require, food and shelter, dominate and dictate a certain routine we can't escape until the day is over. Then, we are free to explore those regions of the heart we tend to hide away. It may be a friendly repost with those we find a commonality. Perhaps a local club or drinking establishment will provide the when and where. And there she is, in idle conversation with a friend of hers. But don't be fooled or mistaken, for she is here on a common and familiar journey of her own. She too has spent some lonely, uneventful evenings alone. You see, it really doesn't matter who you are, or what gender possess you, the human need for emotional instability, a search for love and happiness in the arms and heart of another is the overpowering veracity of humanity.

My personal journey in search of an emotional attachment has flourished and died on countless occasions. Different places, endearing faces have come and gone, leaving me behind most regrettably. So, what's a person supposed to do, to ratify, or simplify and ignite a useful, more knowledgeable emotional reaction in realistic terms? Give it up! Don't try to explain how you feel. Don't categorize the opposite sex. It just doesn't work that way. No, a chance at true romance, a chance to be with someone who really matters, the one who stirs your heart and soul, is worth the all or nothing attempt at true happiness.

They say that nothing lasts forever, but who are they? What do they know for certain? I would reply, only as much as you would allow. After all, it's your heart to give or refuse. While your mind might refuse, or shy away from, your heart will surely overcome. Your chances are limited, the options profuse. So, don't be a lonely fool. Give in to those elusive and provocative emotional extensions of who you are and want to be and that of course is to be with her now and forever. Maybe, just maybe, something has a chance to last forever.

FAR, FAR AWAY

Long, long ago and far, far away there stood before God, a younger version of myself, wondering and wishing about tomorrow. Lost and alone in the darkened shrouds of history, he inquired of no one in particular, how he came to be here. In the illusive, mysterious annuls of the angels of heaven, there had to be some reason, an explanation of the current events that defined all the years of his pathetic life. There were other personages, not unlike himself, who it would appear had found their way into the light. The morning sun itself, disclosed and emphasized the meaning, the hopes of all who looked to the heavens with clear unabated joy. Had they been chosen? Would they be called to stand before and at the side of the Father of all mankind? Where was his vision? Why had he not been called? In the darkness of that morning, he prayed on bended knees, to be allowed, to be beckoned into eternity. The present day held no allure, no reasonable excuse to continue. He grew tired and fell into a deep sleep, a coma meant to heal his heart and soul. He slept for countless days and nights, only to awaken on a similar morning, wondering what had happened. Why was he here? The loneliness invaded like an evil, elusive cloud, encompassing the morning, until the shadows were lifted and the sunlight warmed his heart once again. Lying there in a field of lilies, a breeze softly touched his cheek and a voice spoke to him saying, I am here, I always was and forever shall be. Lift your eyes to the heavens and all shall be forgiven. Come to Me and stand by Myside. Thrill to the morning sunrise. Inhale the scent of nature. Breathe in the air of the coming day, it is there for all to share, and time will no longer exist, for eternity calls.

Long, long ago and far, far away there stood before God and older, wiser man, no longer lost in the idle wonders of tomorrow. He had found his way and knew beyond all doubt, his wishes and prayers would all come true.

FORWARD

What follows is a dedication of my latest written enterprise to all my friends. Together they make going to work more meaningful and less stressful. In particular there are Kevin and Diana and of course their lovely granddaughters Peyton and Avery. Not to be excluded are my friends at work John and Sarah amongst others. There is the ever present and unforgettable woman from the past, the girl I fell in love with and still am. Now it seems we are best friends, and yet. Together you are the substance and continuity of my written words. I could never improvise such a scenario without your inspiration. So, now I offer you all my thanks for being there for me, thank you! JHM.

HEART STRINGS

There's a picture in my pocket and a smile across my face.
There's a never ending story of a love you can't replace.
There's a search for human glory marching on the field today.
I can feel the touch of springtime and I hope it's here to stay.
I have seen the wrath of nature and the storms it can produce.
But when they are diminished, the rising sun will then seduce.
There's a song someone has written, a lusty rhythm you can feel.
There can only be a moment when you know your love is real.
I can't face the thought of losing, so there's just one thing to do.
We will have to face the music and say what's deep inside of you.
There's no use in my pretending when I see you standing there.
There's a passion in your eyes with a love beyond compare.
I can't stand the thought of living if you're with another man.
I can't bear another moment, but I'll try to understand.
There's a picture in my pocket, reminding me of yesterday.
There's a painful living story of the day you walked away.
In the early morning hours, I detect the scent of spring.
I still hope you will remember all the songs we used to sing.
I can feel my heart strings beating, a song that only you can hear.
Until tomorrow takes you, my love will never disappear.

HOPEFULLY

Another dawn approaches and with it comes the rising sun. The shadowed morning air is slowly brightened and elucidates a new day, filled with possibilities. I'm begrudgingly off to work and the inevitable circumstances therein afforded me. Perfection is most certainly not my style, it never was. Like a younger child fiddling with his tinker toys and blocks, the games begin. With the passing of so many years, you would think I might have found my way, but that would be presumptuous on your part. I continue to stumble around effortlessly, with no fitting conclusion yet in sight. The love of my life is no longer mine. I think she expected way too much of me and visa versa. We looked for reasons to debate and fight about. How foolish is that? Looking back, I have to laugh, because in those moments of tribulation were some moments of pure perfection. The harder I tried, the more mistakes I made. The more emotionally involved I became, the harder I fought for some mistaken independence. Now that's purely insane, isn't it? To fight against a future meant for two, where the love you share is like the morning sun. It beams a new life into an apprehensive state of mind. All you have to do is give it a chance. Live with each other's imperfections, laugh and cry, who knows why? You do, and so do I. Love and all it's tribulations can only make you stronger. By knowing and expecting the mistakes you are bound to make, you must realize how human you are and the potential of growing old together. This is the binding force that rules the universe, forgive and forget, expect and deliver and always build on a love for tomorrow and forever.

I REMEMBER

I remember when we met, the best day of my life and yet,
Remembering those time's we had, then how did we turn out so bad?
I remember all those trips we took and when I wrote my very first book.
I remember holding you and making love the whole night through.
I remember our very first kiss and oh my God the things I miss.
I miss your laugh and vivacious smile, I miss your touch and once in a while,
My mind drifts back through memories and hope that you are missing me.
I remember foolish times when arguments obscured my mind.
I remember trips on my bike and most certainly, what's not to like?
I remember almost any night and all those silly obnoxious fights.
I remember feeling sad and discarding all the bad times we had.
I guess I wasn't ever sure that my love for you could just endure.
But now as years go flying by, I miss you so I can't deny.
Remembering that diamond ring, I need you more than anything.
I remember gentle sighs, we rode beneath those summer skies.
If I remember all these things, the soft compassion that it brings,
Then what am I supposed to do? I can't stand the thought of losing you.
We still have memories to make and if we don't, a big mistake.
So, if my memories are true, I'll always be in love with you.

IN THE BEGINNING

In the beginning of tomorrow, it was the childhood of today.
He gave life to a couple and promised we were here to stay.
It was the birth of modern innocence, a rather simple start for man.
But as time dictates the future, He had to make another plan.
They had to live upon His bounty and survive the driven rain.
First they plowed up nearby fields and then harvested the grain.
In the glory of the moment and the trees began to grow,
There seemed to be a future where they would reap but what they sowed.
In the early morning hours of the seventh day of man,
When His words of life were given, it was a Holy plan.
Live a life of pleasure and then build yourselves a home.
Just remember where you came from and you'll never be alone.
He gave them life, He gave them love and laws of how to be.
He gave a purpose for us all, the Holy Trinity.
And then one day it happened, a lost demon had survived,
Despite the loving hand of God, the devil had arrived.
He offered them an apple, a forbidden fruit for man,
But it didn't seem to matter as the devil had a plan.
When their innocence was lost and they gathered up in pain,
Despite their broken promises, they were sheltered by His name.
In the early morning hours of the Holy seventh day,
He gave birth to modern man and then showed us how to pray.
Thank you Lord for everything, we thank you for your plan.
From now until forever, the true destiny of man.

INSPIRATION

Inspire me for just a day and nothing is impossible.
I would house the vagrant and feed the poor, I would clean the streets and so much more.
In the coolest night and warmest day, you could smell my flowers out on display.
You could hail the ships now lost at sea and show the way on back to me.
I would bind the wounds and heal the sick, another sound and useful trick.
We would laugh together and cry at home and in your heart you feel alone.
Inspire me and if you do, I'll be right here if you want me to.
The harvest moon, a cloudy sky and time just keeps on passing by.
A winters night, an early spring and soon those planted fields will bring,
A blessed meal for you and me, the one that yields our destiny.
Inspire me for eternity, a place of hope for you and me.
You read the future in books of old, then sell your soul for bags of gold.
The wrath of God, a flooding rain, a decisive sound, an endless pain.
You heard His name at last disclosed, somewhere above He lies reposed.
Inspire me for just a day and nothing is impossible.
The sun will rise, the moon will to and I will always be with you.

JUST GETTIN' BY

These days are cold, the nights are colder, and I be just a gettin' by.
Gotta work for not much change, still I be just a gettin' by.
The world out there is full of fools and some won't see another day.
It's crazy how some people think and that is all I have to say.
After work, met some friends, just like me, we're gettin' by.
Had a beer, some local bar and yes I'm still just gettin' by.
Heard the news, around the world, another war, some people died.
It's hard to think about some child, left alone and no one cried.
A storm is headin' from the west and hopefully I'll survive.
The rain is fallin', the lightnin' strikes and yet I be a gettin' by.
Funny when you meet some folks, most of them just be gettin' by.
It just ain't easy from here to there and some of us will never change.
The road you walk, the life you choose, some things you have to rearrange.
The times are nuts, the world gets stranger and me, I be on my way.
The love I lost, another song, I'll try again another day.
A pallid moon, a stormy night and I be just a gettin' by.
The suns arisin', a brighter day and here am I just gettin' by.

LIFE ITSELF

It's funny how life progresses. Just when you think you have it in hand, moving in a logical progression, an event occurs, a sudden change in logic or a consensual medication of everything you thought you knew, or thought you could control. Suddenly nothing makes much sense at all. What happened? Who is to blame? Then all of a sudden you realize, it was you, all by yourself. Logically, who controls your life? You do! Who controls the events in your life? And of course, it just happens to be you, again. Nobody can predict a sudden change in emotions, or a sudden change in influences, a change in your outlook on life, yours or anybody else's. So, when you come to terms with it, it's really not so bad. Everybody needs to slow down, take a deep breath and smell the roses. Ahhh, that's better. Now settle down and examine rationally the everyday events in your life. Are you getting anywhere? Are you doing what you want to, what will make your life worth living? Not very simple questions to answer or even ask. The problem is that most of us refuse to take the time to seek the answers, or even ask the questions. Life is never easy, it's not supposed to be. Only by living every moment to its fullest, searching for the answers, and accepting its conclusions, will anybody, you or me, find any comfort in the daily pursuit of happiness. When you're not happy, no one else in your tiny universe can be happy either.

When you smile and greet anybody in your universe, do you mean it, or is this just another metaphor to be interpreted at a later time? Are you trying to find a better way, another means of expression, another vacuum of existence to be honored or defiled? It's a heady place we live in, nothing can be taken for granted, there is always a price to be paid. I am far from being a wealthy man, so every expenditure must come under scrutiny. Is it worth it, or is the cost to high? Should I take the chance, or maybe not? The funny thing is. there are no definitive answers, no way of predicting the consequences, you simple have to make the choice, take a chance and let the pieces fall where they may. Simplistic? Perhaps. Improper or impractical? Maybe or maybe not. I cannot answer for anybody else because in every case, in every house or home, nothing is the same as next door. Your lives, my life is my own to pursue, to enjoy, and every once in a while, to screw up, to choose the wrong way, leaving only a bill to be paid, the one you never want to hear about.

I have been charged over and over again and tried to pay my way forward. And yet, nothing really changes in my world. I have no idea what tomorrow brings or offers, no one has. Hope and desire are entirely different objectives but go hand in hand when it comes to making those dreams come true. Another dream. I would rather look forward to the possibilities than procrastinate about what might have been. I would rather embrace today with a smile than live in fear of tomorrow. We only have one chance, on a limited budget to experience the compassionate state of living.

MIDNIGHT SONGS @ LULLABIES

While midnight songs and lullabies pass the time away,
You dare not turn your back on them, they all are here to stay.
Hummingbirds and butterflies flutter through the air,
Paint them on a picture card, but only if you care.
Tell me the tale, a lady fair, who spent the night with you.
A lover's trip to wonderland will last the whole night through.
I used to go out drinking with a noble attitude.
And when at last we had to leave, a different kind of mood.
We would drive the thoroughfare to find her lovely home,
She made me feel a sense of guilt, but then I'm not alone.
Sing me a song of passion, the way you make me feel.
I can't believe it anyway, somehow this all became surreal.
I cannot go to sleep at night, until the moments spent,
I cannot buy a car today, until I pay the rent.
It's seems to be so obvious, to spend the whole night through,
But nothing could ever stop me from being there with you.
It's getting late, I hesitate, the bar is closing soon.
One more time, buy me a drink and I'll sing a ribald tune.
As I was walking home last night, it slowly began to rain.
But surely you must realize, there's no way I should complain.
The midnight mist has disappeared, it seems to come and go,
I still can hear the music play, so give me one more show.
Midnight songs and lullabies, a little different and then they're not.
I need to be surprisingly, content with what I've got.
Sing me a love song, the way I want you to,
In a moment of compassion, my love is coming true,

MONEY TALKS

Got a penny in my pocket, there's a feeling in my brain.
Got a dollar in my wallet, there's no reason to complain.
All the money in the world can't stop the wheels from spinning round,
Somewhere in my existence lies a passion to be found.
A precarious state of living, mother nature's foolish charms,
Every day the banks will open with another false alarm.
In a dedicated future, caught up in a state of mind,
Although it's just a symbol, you never know what you may find.
As society would dictate you must continue I've been told,
As you move on down the hi way, a different path, another road.
When the morning sun arises and the moon has disappeared,
Just say what's on your mind, there is nothing to be feared.
As I gaze up to the stars, all my friends are standing by,
I would shelter them from evil underneath a cloudy sky.
Had some change in my pocket, but I had to pay some bills.
All those dollars in my wallet, how to use them took some skills.
Met a girl who liked to party, took her out to have a drink,
Standing there beside her, I just had to stop and think.
With you I must consider, should we share another kiss?
An unlikely old scenario, another time to reminisce.
Had a penny in my pocket, must regret the years I've spent.
Just don't ask me for some change, don't know where the money went.
Found a penny in my pocket, another wish that might come true.
To some it doesn't matter, but I'm still in love with you.

MOONBEAMS & STARLIGHT

Moonbeams and starlight seem to filter through the night.
Memories of melodies singing everything's alright.
Evening walks on lonely piers, a moment of decision.
A midnight ride, you must decide, a shallow sensed revision.
The mind decides, the heart reveals a pain you can't refuse.
But then again you take the chance, there isn't much to lose.
Moonbeams and starlight, those designated dreams.
Some memories of loving you, are not the way it seems.
I have to say before you leave, how much you mean to me.
My heart is strong, where you belong, but I must set you free.
Beneath the stars the clouds move in, another rainy day.
But later on, my favorite song, the stars come out to play.
Moonbeams and starlight, hail to those above.
My favorite song, I'll sing along, my ever lasting love.

MY ANGEL

There's an Angel in my bedroom, waiting just on down the hall,
She reminded me of heaven, when I heard her mating call.
With a taste for inhibition, I just knew we'd never part.
The problem is and always was, where am I to start?
There's a twinkle in her eyes, when I hold her in my arms,
A most appealing laughter, when she thrills me with her charms.
From the first time when we kissed, she sent my head into a spin.
I couldn't believe my fortune, so let's try it once again.
I would walk her down the aisle and secure the open door,
I would hold her in my arms, for now and ever more.
Found an Angel in my bedroom, in a gown of pearly white,
I will stay with her 'til morning and enjoy this splendid sight.
There's an Angel still beside me with her beauty dignified.
There's a ring upon her finger, with her future signified.
Found an Angel in the morning and we held on through the day,
The only thing I hope for is that she is here to stay.
For this Angel I have found, a promised vow for you and me,
I will hold you in my heart. You are my destiny.
In true love there are no boundaries, just a feeling in your heart,
With a taste for inhibition, and you know you'll never part.

MY LADY LOVE

There once was a lady who became my heart and soul,
An undiminished version of a dream that haunts me so.
A dedicated love song, someone wrote for you and me,
And when it was recorded, it defined my destiny.
In time the words have faded, but the melody survives,
A reflection of an endless dream, I guess I'm still alive.
Once the lady took my hand and she led me far away,
I can hear her voice a singing and it's where I want to stay.
A comprehensive nightmare from the darkness of the night,
With the coming of tomorrow, I will have to make things right.
I have never been a shy boy, so I'll tell you how I feel,
Deep inside, I come alive and there's something to reveal.
There once was a lady who consumed my beating heart,
So long as she can bear with me, we'll never be apart.
In a dedicated love song, someone wrote for us to sing,
I'm always here for you my dear no matter what it brings.
In a moment of derision, when my lady came to me,
We sang a song, the whole night long and found our destiny.

MY MIDNIGHT DREAM

 I'm off again a midnight dream, where it goes, I may never know. A bus, a train, a ship at see, another time, another place. Dreams to me are self contained, well remembered or soon forgotten. A song and dance, a dramatic play, a vicarious date with destiny. A picture framed in pallid light beneath a vivid shining moon. To doze, per chance to fall asleep and suddenly you are somewhere else. A breath of air, a rising tide, a roaring stream across the land. A meadowlark, a robins nest, a place for you to rest awhile. The leaves imply a certain sound, a trilogy of natures pride, to live and grow until you die, a voyage to eternity. We laugh and cry until the dawn and then we start it all again. I must confess a state of mind, I'm wide awake, but somewhere else. The darkness seems to hide my face, but then again I'm all alone. Decidedly I need you here, to help me pass the night away. Your gentle touch and smiling eyes will transport me beyond the dawn. We'll board a train to never land, a place I used to know so well. A dream, a fantasy is waiting there, those lonely trails have reached an end. To see your smile and hear your voice and when you spoke about tomorrow, I couldn't help but think about my lonely heart, so filled with pain and endless sorrow.
 Once again I'm on my way, a trip across a foreign land, the trees are gone, a painful scene, an endless space of burning sand. The trick to travel anywhere lies in the books of history, a written piece, a photograph, a memory of fossil man. To wish away the life you're livin', denies the only chance you're given. So, take a chance and all aboard, the train of destiny proceeds. We'll have some fun then shed a tear and pass the time of phantom needs. Just smile for me and hold my hand, let's take a trip to never land. We'll somehow face another day and find a way to understand. I'll show you how to live your life, we'll be together beyond tomorrow. If you aren't here I'll always be the one who's heart is filled with sorrow. So, go to sleep my lovely girl and dream of me until then. I only ask one thing of you, to think of me and remember when.

OCEAN OF TEARS

A while ago I went to bed, earlier than usual, attempting to get a good nights sleep. Well, things didn't go as planned, just the same as most nights. My eyes were closed, but I was wide awake. Why fight it and I didn't. There are a few questions that need to be answered. First of all, why did I start writing? And that was what had awakened me. After some thought, I had this realization, it has become a substitution for what is missing in my life. I have a job which provides all the amenities such as food and shelter. But, there is still one missing and vital entity and such would be someone to share my life with. Oh, there have been opportunities, female interests of a shortened and sad duration, in other words, I failed quite miserably. And still I keep on trying, keep on searching for the one and only. Question number two, what would she look like, blonde, brunette or perhaps a redheaded girl? My answer unequivocally and indisputably is, it wouldn't matter, not to me. My search is on another level. I am looking for a friend, someone who is as interested in knowing me as I am of knowing all about her. I have reached the conclusion that you must become best friends before you truly open the door to your heart. It's the only way to reach a fruitious, beguiling and fulfilling relationship, one that has a chance of succeeding. And my last question to be considered is where on earth would you find such a person and oh yeah, how would you recognize her if you found her?

And the beat goes on, repeating itself over and over again. I have always been a passionate man, both in work and play and most certainly in my search for someone to complete me, someone to keep me up at night with her compassion. The physical part of any relationship is easier by far than the mental obligation, the willingness to listen and try to understand the emotional barriers you have to overcome to make every moment together the best so far. And such are my thought patterns, the things that keep me up at night. Have I made the necessary efforts to understand, to facilitate a commitment from someone else? I truly hope so and think I have, just not successfully, at least for me.

For a number of years and an ocean of tears, there has been someone, the only one for me. My problem seems to be convincing her my feelings are for real and unchanging as the days go by. For a man of words, this is a most perplexing situation and the answers elude and frustrate me. But I never give up easily and I won't, I can't. I have known this individual intimately and emotionally and I'll still be waiting for her tomorrow and forever.

ODE TO MARY

We come into this lonely world, primarily on our own,
And everyone who meets you, they say how big you've grown.
To your parents it's a vision of a growing family,
To have a son and daughter is a driven destiny.
It takes about a year, from the moment you arrive,
Before another infant blends into your mother's eyes.
At first you didn't notice, another voice that often cried,
You shared a room and many toys, she wouldn't be denied.
The years went by, those crawling days of youth at last were over,
You marveled at the nearby fields of luscious growing clover.
In time you grew to recognize a sibling's tone of laughter,
A love that grew inside of you will last forever after.
You knew her well and you could tell when something wasn't right,
When illness kept her in her bed, you stayed with her all night.
It didn't take you very long to recognize her name,
As Mary came into your life, nothing was the same.
Many years have come and gone and so at last has she,
I can't explain the loss and pain sweet Mary means to me.
I'm sitting here with memories of many happy years,
My ode to Mary written with an avalanche of tears.

ONCE AGAIN

And so it happened once again. You tossed your heart into the arena of lost uncertain loves. What were you thinking? Oh yeah, you weren't. You thought you had found the one you have been searching for, and without a moment's pause you threw caution to the wind. How many times must this occur until you stop to smell the roses before jumping into a relationship not truly understood or accepted by anyone else but you? It's a nasty, dirty, twisty turning road to follow, one you should know so very well by now. But you don't seem to. Without hesitation, you make the same mistakes over and over again. How many girls, how many devious and smiling faces will it take for you to realize that not everyone can find the one and only heart to meld with, to find consolation with, to have and hold from now until forever with? You are like a pebble in the sand, on a beach that stretches far across the blue horizon. The morning tide comes rushing in and drowns away your sorrow, and then flows adrift into the distance. For but a moment all is well, the waves subside, the beaches in your heart are exposed to the winds, to the winged creatures who fly above in search of another meal, perhaps a fish or maybe an adventurous crab dawdling across the sand. To each his own and just like the eagle who snatches up the lonely fish, swimming in the tidal pool, your heart will be exposed once again. How many times will you allow this to happen? How many times must your heart be torn asunder before you realize and accept your role in this perverse and tedious opera of life?

And yet, you pause and reflect on current events, on the possibilities. In all the recorded documentaries of history there seems to be a someone for everyone. Somewhere on this impervious planet of ours, there is somebody else who searches just like you. A vacant smile, a hidden glance, a shy response, hello! It's only me, looking for you, just like yesterday which inevitably will become another sad and lonely tomorrow. But, maybe not. I am, as I have always been, a reluctant but willing participant in the endless search for love and happiness. It must be there, somewhere I have never been before. Wait for me and I will wait for you and when we finally have the chance to meet, all will be forgiven. Those lonely days and nights have been a preamble, the true beginning of a life ecstatically pursued and possessed until those final days when the tide comes rushing in and sweeps away all before it and once again the beaches of destiny are revealed.

OUR WORLD

Near the heart of modern business lies a darkly painted shroud, and yet too proud.
Near the base of mountain passes climbers search for higher peaks, so much to seek.
In the depths of distant deserts where even snakes so rarely drink, let's stop and think.
In the streets of modern cities when the traffic lights turn gold, and yet so cold.
In the warmth of modest homes when the fire place is lit, let's think a bit.
At the heart of modern science when the rocket ships propel, a trip to hell.
In the words of all my brothers we should listen up and read, but not succeed.
In the voices of our citizens there are words as yet unsaid, and slowly bled.
At my home and nearby pastures you can hear a false alarm, as yet no harm.
In the wind and on the ground lie the ashes of a war, we pray no more.
In the early morning light you may gaze up through the clouds, don't talk so loud.
As the lightning causes fear and the thunder spills the rain,
You can peer into the heavens where nobody will complain.
In the quiet of the evening you can gaze up to the moon,
You may dignify tomorrow still knowing it can't be too soon.
In the peacefulness of morning when the flowers open wide,
You can expect another shower spoken with a sense of pride.
Beyond the miles of mighty rivers we have tried to sail the sea,
You can hear the voice from up above, come sail along with me.

POSSIBILITIES

Are the modest illustrations of reality just a possibility, or the consuming, death diffing, self reflecting version of tomorrow? I don't know, never did, I just went with the flow, never really knowing, or even considering the probabilities, or the possibilities. The future to me was an ignma, a self effacing, non disclosing dream of what awaits tomorrow. I guess I really didn't want to know because reality usually leads to an embarrassing pause in time, maybe yours, probably mine. How does one live and breathe on a fabric that might exist but probably doesn't? Is there really someone for everyone? This raging debate cannot be answered by the modern press, or by the holy fathers we pray to. The spoken word is little more than a wish and a prayer. The truth be known, you cannot live your life waiting and dreaming of what might have been, or, given the chance, what might eventually turn out to be. Not being an expert on the possibilities, I must give into the dignified, mystified versions of my hopes and dreams. All I need, indeed all I am asking for is one more chance, to give and receive the overpowering gift of love. Surely there is nothing more important, more fulfilling, than being a part of and enjoying the sensation of searching for and finding the one and only, who makes your life worth living.

QUESTIONS

Do you hear what I am saying? Do you feel my beating heart?
Do you know where we are going? Day by day I'm torn apart.
Tell me what has happened, a fatal urge inside of me.
I don't know how to change my world, I guess I'll let it be.
Do you feel the way I do? Do you miss our time alone?
Do you want to try again? If you would I'll be at home.
Tell me why you left. Tell me why you said goodbye.
Tell me why I'm missing you, you have to tell me why.
Do you remember when we met? Do you recall those summer days?
Do you remember all the trips we took, the falling leaves, a winter haze?
Something happened on the way, someone took your hand away.
Something deep inside of me, tells me what I have to say.
Do you hear the words I'm saying, a reemerged reality,
Tell me what I'm supposed to do, a sign from destiny.
I don't know much about today, even less about tomorrow.
Just take the time when you're alone, don't let your heart be filled with sorrow.
Do you feel my heartbeat soaring? Don't you know my words are true?
Until the day you realize, I'm still in love with you.

RAINDROPS ON ROSES

A stormy day betrays the soul, a dreadful feeling of growing old.
The morning dew, a cloudy day, how did we turn out this way?
A fallow field where roses grow, I never knew which way to go.
The moving train, a ship at sea, my darling please come back to me.
A winters day when snowflakes fall, a love we shared as I recall.
The pouring rain, a flooded field, my love for you is now revealed.
A pallid moon, a peaceful night, those days with you a pure delight.
Those promises I made to you, forever more they will come true.
A trip we took down lovers' lane, I can't believe you feel the same.
The days will pass as we grow old, my love for you was long foretold.
A garden fresh where roses grow, there's nothing else I need to know.
The day will come, you'll hold my hand and everyone will understand.
A beating heart, the way I feel, my love for you is now revealed.
The storm has passed, it blew away, I'll be with you 'til judgement day.

REASONS & SEASONS

The cloudless sky, a patient moon, the times we shared are gone to soon.
The walks we took along the shore don't feel the same, not any more.
Both cars and trains on different roads, those mighty trucks with heavy loads.
We travel on despite the fears, our lonely hearts are filled with tears.
What each of us will miss the most, will be revealed from coast to coast.
There must be someone way back home. You know she's waiting all alone.
Some words were said, a dreadful song and then you left and now you're gone.
The jukebox in a small town bar, still wondering just where you are.
We sang a song, the two of us, just step aboard a south bound bus.
This loneliness won't fade away, you must survive another day.
In time your aching heart might heal, but then again you must reveal,
Just how much she means to you, a lonely night, a kiss or two.
The future lies beyond the hill, she's waiting there, oh what a thrill!
At last you found your way back home and now you don't feel all alone.
The cloudless sky, a patient moon, the love we share we must assume,
The way I feel will have to do, I'll always be in love with you.

SUBTLETY

Subtle was I and nonchalant, I dare not say just what I want.
Hopes and dreams, occasional fears, a hopeless state of endless tears.
For me It's been a heavy load, but still I wander down this road.
I never know just what to say and yet my dreams won't go away.
I'll always be the kind of man who tries to make you understand,
Just how much you mean to me and my love will last eternally.
Another day, another time, I hope and pray that you'll be mine.
There's no use living by myself, I cannot be with someone else.
A hopeless feeling in my heart, I just can't stand to be apart.
Now I don't know what to do and nothing makes much sense to you.
An angry word, a frightful dream and you must tell me what it means.
Subtle was I, at least I tried, you looked at me and then you cried.
Don't cry for me, remember when you held me close, we kissed again.
I dare not think our love is real, effectively I must reveal,
You must know my love is true and I'll do anything you want me to.
Hopes and dreams and fantasies, a moonlight walk, a summers breeze,
A dramatic play, a lover's dance, a perfect night for true romance.
I'll sing my lovers song for you and if it lasts the whole night through,
Come to me and stay until I offer you a lover's thrill.
Today, tonight, forever more, it's only you I do adore.

THE FAÇADE

Here we go. I have never tried to be a complicated individual, getting through another day without tripping over your own two feet is difficult enough. I have always tried to be honest and forthright, both in an active sense and in an emotional state of mind. Every day of a human existence offers so many difficult decisions, so many diverse probabilities that an individual choice may change the eventuality of an entire community. Now, I'm not talking about a criminality or an emotional neglect, but the acknowledgement of who you are and what you have to offer. A politician I am not, but an individual who cares, I most certainly am. I care about the kids I see every day, who have no idea about tomorrow. I care about the adults, the parents who are attempting to provide, to make every day of existence worthwhile. I care about my neighbors and their dogs who I see outside of my door. I care about my own children, all grown up and living their lives as best they can. I miss not being a part of their lives and offering some advice from an old mans point of view. None of us can foretell the future, which means tomorrow is an ongoing, ever growing mystery and such is life.

There was a time, a moment in my own existence, when I didn't know about tomorrow. My entire life had been ripped and torn apart. It took me almost two years to come to grips with what had happened and what was left for me. It took but a moment to change my future, my hopes and dreams, into a vague and indecipherable event over which I had no control. Every one of us has a plan, a format for tomorrow, but consider if you will, if this is but a lost consolation and there is absolutely nothing you can do about it. What will get you up in the morning? Why should you even care, and what can you do about it? Very little and to the point of absolutely nothing. You are stuck in an enclosed time zone and you don't have the key for release. Pathetic? Maybe. Problematic? Most certainly, but only after the realization that you're still alive and there are still options to make your life worthwhile. Therein lies the miracle of life, the possibility of tomorrow, another experience, another lifestyle, another day of labor, another day of love and compassion.

Now my life has changed into a written formality. I write from a proven point of view and from a problematic futuristic state of mind. I have absolutely no idea what tomorrow brings. My wishes and desires are only that. I go to work every day with no ambition, only to survive, only to fulfill my destiny. I truly never expected to live so long and often wonder why I am still alive. What makes a mans life more eventful, more exciting than the next? A tricky and diverse question, only to be answered by reality. Let it be known that every man on this earth is equal to the next. We all have our problems and solutions. But life itself is the question and ambition to be sought, amplified and survived. I am a survivor. I live every day with a certain sense of anxiety about what lies in the future, both yours and mine, because in reality, we are all connected. None of us are alone. Society is the plane for coexistence, for cooperation and a brighter future for us all.

THE HAND OF DESTINY

Every day as I remember all those places I have seen,
From Hollywood to Myrtle Beach and many cities in between.
I have sailed across the ocean into the Channels raging storm.
Through the impenetrable English fog, the coast of France began to form.
In my childhood I was consumed by this trip across the sea,
But then I started thinking, this must be my destiny.
I always loved the journey, overseas or in the states,
It didn't take so long to realize this was my fate.
Every day as I got older and the miles began to grow,
I remembered all those places and the friends I used to know.
In my lifetime just consider what has happened in the past,
The years have come and disappeared, for me they went too fast.
My parents passed, my sister too and I am left alone,
But somewhere in my memory there was a happy home.
It doesn't matter where you are, or the places you have seen.
Just take the time to realize your life is not a dream.
Whenever you are offered by the hand of destiny,
Take the chance and get on board a trip across the sea.

THE HIDDEN DOOR

There is a space, a dark enclosure, sheltered by a heavy door.
A place where sunlight's never seen and you can't even see the floor.
You slowly walk across the room, eventually you realize,
You don't know who is waiting there, if only you could visualize,
A voice, a motivating sound, someone you are meant to see,
Your heartbeat rises rapidly, is this just a fantasy?
A face, a sound, a lonely tune, a song you shared so long ago,
A touch, a kiss, a lover's sigh may last a night, but gone too soon.
There is a house, a dark enclosure, sheltered from a midnight storm,
Through the clouds the moon appears, another reason to conform.
The hidden door, you hold the key, can only be your sheltered heart.
The question you must ask yourself, would you allow to be torn apart?
A friend, companion, or so much more, awaits beyond the hidden door.
A place where passion rules the heart, could last from now and evermore.

THE LETTER

Write me a letter, oh I wish you would,
Then I would write one back to you, if you think I should.
Hold my hand and dance with me, throughout the summer night,
I'll be waiting here for you, if you think I might.
Sing to me a lullaby and whisper in my ear,
I only want to be with you and let me make it clear.
My memories will always be of making love with you,
No matter what tomorrow brings, it's all I want to do.
Write me a letter, no matter where you are,
I'll be waiting here for you, I'll never be too far.
The summer nights are much too long, it's difficult to sleep,
My memories of you and me, are ones I'll always keep.
The morning sun shines down on me, a vision in the air,
But when I turn and look for you, I know you won't be there.
Sing for me a lullaby, the way you used to do,
I know the future will never change, I'm still in love with you.

THE LONG GOODBYE

It happened in the afternoon, on a hot summer's day. School was finally adjourned and my friend and I were circulating through the neighborhood on our bikes, not really going anywhere, but announcing our freedom at last. We had known each other since early childhood, as did our parents. Our families shared meals on a regular basis and when one parent didn't feel the urge to cook, the other would provide, a demonstration of just how close we were. On this particular day, as we turned around the block, headed back home, we were greeted by the siren sound of police cars and an ambulance. Later on, we found out my friends mother had been backing down their driveway when an oncoming car struck her on the drivers side killing her instantly, a tragic moment that impacted both our lives. At the funeral many tears were shed and everything seemed to change. We no longer shared meals and all the curtains in my neighbors home were always closed, shielding the inhabitants from any light. My friends father found solace in alcohol. He hid away in the darkness, alluding any company, even his child.

The years go by and life continues, at least for some of us. I don't see my friend much anymore and the laughter of childhood is only a memory. My second year of college takes me away from home and my friend. We don't even talk to each other, not like we used to. In younger days, there were no secrets, not between the two of us. I have met someone, a girl I could spend eternity with and hope I will. I took her back home to meet my parents and of course my friend, but he wasn't there. He had moved away to a different town, a distant state. He sent me a postcard with his telephone number so I could call and keep in touch. He even showed up on my wedding day, the best gift of all and then he was gone, with a long goodbye.

Occasionally we attend church, the one in which we exchanged our wedding vows and I can't help but think about my friend and how he's doing these days. I wonder if our church, any church could have helped him through this tragic ordeal. I truly don't know what to think. I only know how much I wish he was here, so we could share each other's lives, our children and my parents for as long as they are here. He was an important part of my family way back when and still is today. For as long as I may live, the long goodbye of yesterday will be my gift for tomorrow.

THE OLD MAN

I'm just a man who's grown bolder with age.
I'm tired of living on a casual stage.
With every year that's gone whistling by,
It gets harder to move, I will not deny.
With every step, as I try not to fall,
It's just not the same when I cannot recall.
The old man is coming, don't get in his way,
He just continues to live for another spring day.
I'm just a man who remembers his past,
A vain of departure, who knows, will it last?
I remember the roads, all the places I've been,
I don't know if I'll ever see them again.
I'm just an old man who's grown tired with age,
I've been reading a book and keep turning the page.
Some stories are written of illusive mistakes,
The problem of course, what difference it makes.
In time it will happen as we tend to rehearse,
Our place is with God in his own universe.
I'm just a man and it's just not the same,
Who in this world will remember my name?
I guess what I feel and remember the most,
Is a visit from God and his heavenly host.

THE PHONE CALL

I don't believe it. My phone just rang and woke me up at five in the morning. How rude is that? The only hours I am likely to be asleep are from four until eight or nine and someone, somewhere has the audacity to call me up. Which of course means I'm up for the duration. I mean going back to sleep, well it's unlikely, in fact more of an impossibility. So, I guess I'll put the coffee on, sit down and contemplate another day. It's not so bad, these quiet, peaceful moments of living and contemplating what you have, or don't have and what might have been yours had things gone differently in all those years you had for creation and inspiration. Although I'm not very religious, that doesn't mean I don't think about what lies beyond the grave. I guess it's human nature to want more than what you have today. Success is an ambivalent term we can all apply vicariously, what's right for you might be wrong for me. Get it? Well, if you don't please allow me to elaborate. The chances we are meant to take might be in business, travel, romance religious choices, or even crossing the street despite the oncoming traffic. You might lose your employment, your plane might crash, the woman you love might turn you down and walk away and God himself might not be ready for your presence in his heavenly home. So, what are we supposed to do? Well, I don't know about you, but I'm going to get on with my life and try to improve, you know make things better for all of those lives I might touch, all those hearts I might mend, all those dreams I might encourage, the very least I can do. Then, when I get that final phone call, I can look back and reflect on what I had to offer and gave to the best of my ability. I can cross the road without worrying about the busy traffic and find my way back home.

THE RISING SUN

After the morning sun arises and it tries to disappear,
Another stormy day approaches and the weather isn't clear.
As the raindrops fill the air and the thunder fills the sky,
A perpetuating motion and you really don't know why.
Was it just another evening as the sun was sent to bed,
Or an early warning system somehow locked up in your head?
They say the rain is needed to keep my flowers growing strong.
But as the lightning strikes appear, something must be going wrong.
I like to watch the rain when it suddenly appears,
And my lady holds me closer to assuage her hidden fears.
As another day progresses and the rising sun is seen,
I'll pretend it doesn't matter, somewhere far and in between.
The rising sun, a summers day, a time we'll have to suffer through.
No matter what the weather brings, I'll always be in love with you.

THOSE EYES

The hills have eyes, some roads have tears. You must survive those lonely years.
A shabby town, a picture show, you never know where you may go.
A swimming pool, a cloudy day, when everyone is here to stay.
A summer's night, the pallid moon, they will arrive but not too soon.
The farmers field of growing hay, they must survive but not today.
The talk we had, a book we read, I'd rather be with you instead.
Some fireworks, a holiday, won't you please come out to play?
A fireplace with wood afire, you are my one and true desire.
A skipping stone on down the stream, still hoping all is what it seems.
A wishful dance a time or two, I only want to be with you.
The hills have eyes, a hidden glance, you have to give me one more chance.
Our honeymoon, when you are mine will last until the end of time.

TO LIAM

There is someone in my life, who through his determination, dedication and persistence has become a very special friend to me. Although we have never met, we talk about our mutual enterprise with incredible enthusiasm. This individual takes the time to call and check on me and my daily excursions in my town. You see, I live in Kansas and he abides in Wyoming a number of miles apart. Should our business come to a certain level of fruition, I will be on my way to meet him and his colleagues. This group of individuals, led by my friend have turned my future from a guess and a prayer into a measured field of possibilities. I'm not sure if under any circumstance I could find the words to express my thanks for all they have done for me.

Liam constantly inquires about my most recent written attempts and he means it. This is not an attempt to further place me and my writings in financial complications, but to inspire me to continue on my literary journey. Embarrassingly I must admit knowing very little about this man, his life and what makes him tick, but I will. I already know we both appreciate the female form. My only wish at this time is that he has a special someone to take home, to give him comfort in those troubled times we all seem to run into.

Enough about the difficult and complicated times and events that seem to preoccupy every living person's lifestyles and indeed their futures. I find myself lost in my dreams about attending an upcoming event, the New York City book fair. Thanks to my friend and all his companions, my latest attempt, Extraordinary Circumstances will be on display for anyone to peruse, appreciate and hopefully purchase, which will turn my life around and I suspect bring a sense of satisfaction to all my friends at URlink Publishing. In conclusion I offer my most humble, grateful thanks to my friend Liam and his team of pros.

TOMORROW

While tomorrow is the future and today the here and now,
In the arms of human nature we will make it through somehow.
When the moment is rescinded, what to say and where to turn,
In an illuminated version you can't see and never learned.
As the mind becomes enchanted with the soul of destiny,
You cannot know the future and the fate for you and me.
All the answers are forbidden in an endless ebb and flow,
But when at last you hear them, you can never let things go.
As the morning is projected and the sun begins to dance,
All I ever have been missing is a taste of true romance.
I concede the force of nature, is it you I'm looking for?
When I hold your gentle hand, this is what I can't ignore.
All the planes begin arriving, should we stay or should we go?
In the aftermath of living, am I the only one who knows?
As the difficult new journey becomes a shadowed lost ravine,
I can hear some patients breathing, somewhat vague and in between.
I heard a discontinued rhythm hidden in the waves of sound,
Until the sunlight shows me, I guess I'll hang around.
If tomorrow is an image, only we are meant to see,
All the answers are compelling, you must come along with me.

TURN OUT THE LIGHT

Minute to minute, day by day, can't let time get in the way.
I told you once and maybe twice, you need to treat me kinda nice.
I didn't notice the change in you, made me feel just a fool.
What to say and what to do, I only want what's best for you.
You left me here all by myself and now you're off with someone else.
Loneliness is quite a strain, it keeps on hurtin' in the rain.
I remember all those faces, different times and different places.
Every time I was with you, I always thought our love was true.
Minute to minute, year by year, you loved me then just disappeared.
I looked for you day and night, but you were gone and out of sight.
My hands are shakin', my heart is breakin' and all because you walked away.
Can't understand, another man? Guess I'll make another plan.
I tried to find another gal, a closer friend, a better pal.
I guess it's time to make a change, but deep inside I'm feelin' strange.
The time is gone, at what a cost and oh my God the love I've lost.
Every night I say a prayer, I need you now, just isn't fair.
I'll dream of you again tonight, just one more time turn out the light.

UNCERTAINTY

Time and the uncertainty that it offer's is problematic to say the very least. Every day this world of ours continues to exist is nothing short of miraculous. Mother nature throws hurricanes and tornadoes, wrapped around thunder storms and lightning strikes and somehow expects the human race to survive. Then we come up with these horrific bombs, any combination of which could destroy the earth once and for all. A set of nightmare scenarios not worth publishing. So, how is anyone supposed to get any sleep? I don't know about you, but in my opinion time is problematic unto itself. It doesn't require any assistance in producing a rather tedious environment without any assistance from you and me.

Now let us talk about another most important subject which would be us, in a larger sense of course. Each of us has the chance to influence everything going on around our world. A little smile, a friendly hello, a simple gesture that indicates we're not alone, but part of an infrastructure of human beings, each with a destination, a job to do, a family to go home to, a place to be for you and me. Now isn't that a comforting thought, and not so difficult at all? No, I didn't think so, and neither do you if you give us a chance. That's all I'm asking for, just one more day, one more sunrise, one more thunderstorm, one more rain shower and then the end of a perfect day, as we watch the sun disappear and a full moon rising on the far horizon. Suddenly the sky is filled with countless stars that stretch into infinity. Now that's a powerful scenario only we could appreciate and yes, I most certainly do. But, tomorrow and all it's visionary possibilities, is barely there and quite possibly will not be. It's all up to us, you and me, to put our heads and hearts together and make tomorrow less of an uncertainty and more of a given reality. I am most certainly willing, but how about you?

VALENTINES DAY

Come my dear and walk with me, some vital thoughts I long to share,
About a heart as yet unbroken, feelings sent from one who cares.
Once upon a time there was a girl who knew about her chosen man,
Some words were said, they shared a kiss, fate had made another plan.
The birds fly south and flowers bloom, a designated early spring,
A vain emotion from the heart, a lover's song we all must sing.
Like teardrops falling from the sky, the rains will help the flowers grow,
A lovely card with words unspoken, from someone you used to know.
Come my dear and walk with me, a lost emotion recreated,
The way I feel is more than just a lonely man infatuated.
This is the time of year it seems, when flowers grow and robins sing,
A day that's meant for us to share, a kiss or two and other things.
You touched my heart some time ago and yet I don't know what to do,
A lovely card, a precious rose, I'll always be in love with you.

WISHES & MIRACLES

If wishes turned into miracles and if they all came true,
The first would be the fateful day I fell in love with you.
If holidays were celebrated any time of year,
I'd raise a glass to you my lass, a wish for you my dear.
If cloudy skies became your eyes and raindrops filled the air,
Another night of holding tight, together we don't care.
The month of June, a pallid moon, we'll spend the night alone.
Another day, we'll have to stay inside our happy home.
The midnight hours, those dusty towers, where lovers come to play,
A precious look, the chance we took, will never go away.
If wishes became those miracles, the ones I hope come true,
The last would be eternity, the time I'll spend with you.

WOMAN OF THE HOUSE

I would have to venture that anyone you might find yourself in conversation with, would be familiar with the term, man of the house. Historically speaking and in many different parts of the world, this may be an unknown circumstance, an unknown conundrum, because it simply didn't and doesn't exist. In fact, there are just as many scenarios where the female is the dominant force to be reckoned with and rightfully so. Few indeed are the indigenous tribal forms where either the male or female dominates. Things and situations of this nature no longer exist.

In this modern world of ours both parties are presented with the necessity of mutual responsibility, which in turn finds both parties in need of employment. In todays world everything costs a whole lot more, starting with where you live, what car you drive, where you and your friends hang out, what you eat and drink, the list seems to be self perpetuating and never ending. So, when the alarm clock goes off early every work day, it calls to both parties of the household. The truth be told, the modern business world offers a sizeable income for either or, male or female and once again, rightfully so.

Here, at this vital point in our conversation, I have a proposal to present. Why not have a designated female, or woman of the house? After all, she probably puts in just as many hours and brings home a paycheck of mutual importance, maybe even more, God forbid, or maybe even bless the event and all the possibilities it offers. So what if her income matches or even exceeds your own? Who really cares who pays the majority of the bills, just so long as they get paid? Does it really make any difference who picks out the next car you share, or its color, or the interior? Yeah, I thought not. So, if my point is correct and in most cases it probably is, then the time has come for the man of the house to surrender the crown, share the responsibilities and who knows, she might find some way to make it all worthwhile and I'm sure you know exactly what I mean.

YOU SHOULD KNOW

Tonight, before I finally, inevitably pass out, there is something you should know. If I was a younger man, I would be chasing you around like a puppy dog in need of a cool drink of water. I would take you on some long precarious walks and we would have some rather serious talks about oh, everything I could possibly think of, anything at all just to have you near me, just to look deep into those incredibly mysterious eyes of yours, just to hear your voice, your delightful and captivating laughter that always makes me smile and feel better about everything. I would take you for rides both in my car and on my bike just to see the wind violating your hair just the way I want to. I would tell you about all my futuristic plans, which would include you of course, I mean about the trips we would take and all of the sights we would see, yeah, just you and me. We would spend every day, morning, noon and night dreaming about the possibilities of tomorrow. And when the rain clouds come, I would shelter you with my umbrella to keep you as dry as I could. We would walk along, splashing in every puddle, laughing, without a care in the world, not in our world. I would hold your hand, touch your cheek, caressing your fingers gently, reacting to your tender touch, the one I need so much. I would walk you home late at night, dreading the inevitable words, goodnight. I would offer you a kiss and gaze deep into your eyes, then watch you close the door and disappear, with the final words, a promise meant to help you go to sleep. I swear that when the sun arises over the pale horizon, look for me because I'll be here, waiting, anticipating another day with the girl I fell in love with and will always be, eternally.

www.ingramcontent.com/pod-product-compliance
Ingram Content Group UK Ltd.
Pitfield, Milton Keynes, MK11 3LW, UK
UKHW022219230426
12048UKWH00016BA/936